camille Pissarro

Ernest Rouart

Edgar Degas

Julie Manet

Edouard Manet

Paul Marmottan

Claude Monet

Auguste Renoir

Jules Marmottan

Berthe Morisot

Alfred Sisley

Paul Cézanne

Claude Monet

Auguste Rodin

Contents

In the greenery behind Chaillot hill, Christophe Edmond Kellerman, the Duke of Valmy, built a splendid hunting lodge.

A few years later, Jules Marmottan purchased the lodge and bequeathed it, along with all of his belongings to his son Paul. The young man moved into the lodge, and devoted himself to his passion: the history of the Napoleonic era. In addition to his research, he built an important collection. The lodge's galleries could no longer contain all of his paintings, furniture, and bronzes. In the yard, he built a small pavilion dedicated to the Empire. Paul bequeathed his home to the Académie des Beaux-Arts. The Musée Marmottan was born. Opening its doors in 1934, the museum presented a large and eclectic collection of art objects. Over the years, the foundation would receive other fabulous donations.

Madame Victorine de Monchy made the first donation. She left the works that her father, Doctor Georges de Bellio, bought or accepted as a token of appreciation for the care he provided to artists. Thus, the museum was no longer focused on history paintings and portraits from the dawn of the nineteenth century. From the domain of the Consulate and First Empire souvenirs, the museum then became the location that housed the famous *Impression: Sunrise*, which inspired the name for the most celebrated artistic movement of the nineteenth century.

Michel Monet, Claude Monet's youngest son, donated his father's paintings from Giverny, whose magical garden was the most important source of inspiration for the artist. Today, the Musée Marmottan owns the largest collection of Monet's work in the world.

To exhibit the artworks, a large underground room was built. It is similar to the space that Monet wanted to show the *Giant Decorations* that he gave to the State.

The Duhem Collection was bequeathed to the museum by the daughter of the painter, Henri Duhem who carefully selected works by a prestigious group of artists: Boudin, Caillebotte, Carrière, Corot, Gauguin, Monet, and Renoir.

In 1980, an extraordinary ensemble of illuminations collected by Georges Wildenstein was donated by his son Daniel, to enrich the museum.

In 1996, an exceptional donation was received from Annie Rouart. Her husband, Denis Rouart, was Berthe Morisot and Eugène Manet's grandson. Several masterpieces by Degas, Manet, Monet, and Renoir surround those by their friend and counterpart, Berthe Morisot, one of the few female artists of the nineteenth century.

Respecting current museological practices, the museum protects this remarkable ensemble and universal heritage, whose eclecticism of styles and time periods contribute to its originality. The museum presents the most important works from its collections; meanwhile it maintains the original spirit of the site: the exhibition space of a brilliant art lover.

Thirteenth to Sixteenth Century Illuminations
The Wildenstein Collection

In 1980, the Musée Marmottan first exhibited its collection of illuminations donated by Daniel Wildenstein. Exceptional for both the quantity and the quality of the works, the collection consists of more than three hundred miniatures of inestimable artistic and historical worth. Two of the illuminations are from a fifteenth-century manuscript that Nathan Wildenstein offered to his fourteen-year-old son, Georges.

Anonymous
Crucifixion
Paris, ca. 1220
Artist from the Circle of the Moralizing Bibles.
Folio from a missal or a psalter.

William de Brailes
The Fourth Plague of Egypt (insects)
Oxford, 1230-1240
Scene from Genesis. Folio from the Manuscript of the Walters Art Gallery in Baltimore (USA).

Georges Wildenstein was an eminent connoisseur of eighteenth-century art history. Like his father, he combined business expertise, the intellectual abilities of an art lover, and the work of a historian. With patience and passion, through sales and meetings, he formed this *mysterious collection*, whose treasures covered the walls of his office. Thus, his collection unites in one place work from the artistic centers of Italy and France, as well as numerous rare pieces from the Netherlands, Germany, and England. It covers a period of four centuries, from the Middle Ages to the Renaissance.

Belbello da Pavia
Saint Catherine of Alexandria. Initial R
Lombardy, mid-fifteenth century.
Excerpted from a hymnbook, this historiated initial is remarkable both for the material's relief and for the delicacy of its manufacture. This beautiful depiction of the martyred virgin is unparalleled. The artist is well known by historians because of the various works he illuminated for the enjoyment of important patrons such as Filippo Maria Visconti of Milan and Niccolo d'Este.

Created by monks working in the half-light of the scriptorium, illuminations decorated and illustrated books from the Middle Ages, liturgical works, missals, evangeliaries, as well as graduals and antiphonaries. The Christians who owned illuminations believed they were genuine relics.

Jean Perréal
Nature's Lament to the Wandering Alchemist
Known for a long time as Jean de Paris, Pérreal was the official court painter of Charles VIII, Louis XII and François I. He shared the title for a long time with Jean Bourdichon. In particular, he was appreciated for the quality of his small portraits.

Jean Bourdichon
The Kiss of Judas
Tours, late fifteenth century
Folio from a Book of Hours.
Served as the official court painter to four kings: Louis XI, as Jean Fouquet's successor, Charles VIII, Louis XII and François I. He lived from 1457? to 1521. One of his most famous illuminated manuscripts is The Great Hours of Anne of Brittany.
The quality of this folio is remarkable from its composition, to the hatched lines of the drawing, to the colors selected: the deepness of the blues is illuminated by gold flecks, which light the nocturnal scene and give it a brilliant intensity.

Jean Fouquet
Episode in the Life of
Saint Vrain
The Bishop of Cavaillon
Saint Vrain is exorcizing a possessed man in Notre-Dame de Paris. This scene is one of the earliest known representations of the cathedral before the Renaissance. The illumination is from the Hours of Etienne Chevalier (1452-1460), secretary and treasurer of Charles VII of France. This manuscript was painted entirely by the hand of Jean Fouquet, and it is one of the most sumptuous ever executed. Pages were removed from it during the eighteenth century. Fouquet was well known during his lifetime. The illuminations found in this book demonstrate his originality, especially the composition of this folio. It is highly detailed and animated by the distribution of the colors. Fouquet used bright colors for the clothes of the figures located in the foreground, and different shades of dark colors on the stones to enhance the immensity of architecture and the poignancy of the exorcism.

Illuminations evolved over time. This evolution resulted from the use of different media, the development of instruction, the creation of new universities, and a continual exchange of diverse artistic trends. Illuminations would also be used to illustrate secular books.

Sano di Pietro
God Creating the Stars. Initial O
Sienna, fifteenth century
The brilliance of the colors in this initial is extraordinarily well-preserved. The Creator, with the crossed halo of Christ, stands in front of the Earth. He grasps his golden cloak in one hand as though it contained all the stars, which he scattered in the sky with his other hand.

In the thirteenth century, illuminations gained in popularity. It was at this time that royal and aristocratic patrons began to order them. Illuminators expanded their production, bringing sumptuous delicacy to their work.

In addition to liturgical books, powerful patrons desired Books of Hours, inventories, literary works from ancient and modern authors, scientific writings, bestiaries, and herbals. Patrons in France included the Duke de Berry and the Dukes de Bourgogne, and in Italy, important families like the Medicis and the Viscontis.

Thus, illuminators gradually gained artistic freedom, as seen in the composition, the choice of the palette, the architectural décor, and the expression of the figures.

Little by little, images started to occupy their own space, and in the end, they overshadowed the writing they illustrated.

Anonymous
The Liberation of Saint Peter. Initial N
Tuscany, mid-fourteenth century

Master of Salomon Wildenstein
Saint Michael Fighting the Demon
Initial B
Milan, late fifteenth century

Unfortunately, these illuminations have been removed from their original manuscripts, which allows each page to be individually exhibited and admired. Thus, visitors can consider narrative letters or historiated initials, focusing on works by unknown painters or those by some of the most famous ones. Indeed, as early as the late thirteenth century, *an artists' guild* was formed in Paris. Studios directed by unknown artists existed elsewhere. When illuminations could not be attributed to the work of one hand (e.g. The Master of the Gradual of Gand, mid-fifteenth century, Tounai), or identified by their prestigious author (e.g. William de Brailles, thirteenth century, England; Jean Colombe, late fifteenth century, Jean Perréal, a famous painter under Charles VIII, Jean Bourdichon and Jean Fouquet, France), manuscripts were classified by school. These included: Franco-Burgundian, Ghent-Bruges, or, in Italy, the Schools of Florence, Sienna…

French School
The Admiral of Graville Hunting the Wild Boar
Paris, after 1493

Coats of arms of Louis Malet and his two eldest daughters. Miniature on parchment from the manuscript titled "The Terrier of Marcoussis." This inventory ledger also records episodes from the life of an important French lord in his rural domain at the end of the fifteenth century. The great Marcoussis hunts were very prestigious. Kings and princes often participated. In the center of the scene is the admiral, wearing a white hat and gold clothes and riding a handsome warhorse. Around the border and on the bottom of the page are the coats of arms of the family.

At the end of the Trecento in Italy, the art of illumination benefited from new conceptions of space, movement, coming closer to reality and *truth*. This gave rise to the work of the Italian master, Ambrogio di Bondone, known as Giotto. The magnificent productions from the Schools of Flo-rence and Sienna rivaled those of Venice and Lombardy. Until the sixteenth century, some of the most famous artists included Attavante, Lorenzo Monaco, Cristoforo Cortese, Belbello da Pavia, Niccolo di Giaccomo and Giulio Clovio.

Gradually, the ties between illustrations and texts were severed. While manuscript writing was abandoned in favor of modern methods, the images were framed, and their compositions, choices of subject, and means of representation served as a source for easel painting.

Master of the Book
of Prayers of 1500
The Resurrection of Lazarus
Bruges
Folio from a Book of Hours.

Giulio Clovio
The Battle of David and Goliath
Central Italy, ca. 1560
Famous sixteenth-century illuminator, G. Clovio
was often inspired by Michelangelo.

Jules and Paul Marmottan
From the stained glass of Soissons to the sumptuous works of the First Empire

I bequeath to the Institut de France (Académie des Beaux-Arts) my mansion on Avenue Raphaël… for the creation of a museum.

Paul Marmottan donated his entire collection as well as his mansion, which was built at the end of the Second Empire by the Duke of Valmy, to the Académie des Beaux-Arts. He wanted to offer the public a coherent vision of the art of the First Empire by recreating, with the help of archives on furniture and decorative arts, the atmosphere of the era. To present his collection, he enlarged the original architecture of his mansion considerably. Concerned with the accuracy of the renovation, Marmottan referenced *Recueils de décorations intérieures* published in 1812 by architects and decorators Charles Percier and Pierre Fontaine. He redecorated all of the rooms in the style of the First Empire by adding stucco, classical friezes, painted doors, and chandeliers.

Johan Georg Otto von Rosen
Portrait of Paul Marmottan
1899, oil on canvas

◁
The Marmottan mansion seen from Avenue Raphaël.
Archival photograph.

▷
Louis Boilly and Xavier Bidauld
Promenade of Napoleon and Marie-Louise on the Carp Pond at Fontainebleau
1810, oil on canvas
One of six paintings that belonged to Louis Nicolas Davout, Marshal of the Empire, which decorated the paneling of his sitting room in his chateau at Savigny-sur-Orge. The figures that animate Bidauld's landscapes are painted by Carle Vernet or Louis Boilly. The imperial couple is represented in the parks at the chateaux of Fontainebleau, Compiègne, and Saint-Cloud.

Jules Marmottan

Inaugurated on June 21, 1934, the Musée Marmottan also includes the collections of Jules Marmottan, the father of the donor. Born in Valenciennes in 1829, Jules was an industrialist who was the Director of the Mines of Bruay (in Pas-de-Calais), then he became the Treasurer of Gironde. An art lover, he was interested in German, Flemish and Italian primitive painters. Several notable works that he acquired from Antoine Brasseur, an antiques dealer and art restorer from Cologne, include *The Virgin and Child* (ca. 1500) by the Master of Altarpieces of Hohenlandberg, *Scene of Revolt in Rome against the Decemvirs* and a *Crucifixion* by Dirk Bouts from 1536.

A stained glass window from the Soisssons Cathedral, four early sixteenth-century polychromed wooden statuettes from Mechelen, tapestries relating the *History of Saint Suzanne*, pastels and watercolors by Gabrielle Capet and Louis Vigée, as well as a series of gouaches by Jean-Baptiste Mallet complete Jules Marmottan's collection.

The History of Saint Suzanne
French Tapestry, sixteenth century

Stained glass window
Thirteenth century
One of four stained glass panels produced in the region of
Soissons that might be from the windows of the cathedral.

Anonymous, Umbria
*Scene of the Roman Revolt and the Death of Appius
Claudius in 446 BCE*
Sixteenth century, tempera on wood

School of Mechelen
Saint Agnes
Fifteenth century, gilded and painted wood
Saint Agnes is one of four statuettes from Mechelen acquired
by Jules Marmottan. In the fifteenth and sixteenth centuries, the
town of Mechelen in Brabant became an artistic center famous
for the production of altarpieces and wooden sculptures.
The crest of Mechelen, which includes three stakes and the
letter M (for Mechelen), appears on this figurine and the three
others in the collection. The crest certifies the quality of the
wood and the application of the colors.

Michel Haider
The Virgin and Child
ca. 1500, oil on wood

Napoleonic Italy

Giambattista Gigola
*Portrait of the Viceroy of Italy Eugène de Beauharnais
as the Prince of Venice*
Miniature on ivory, 1807-1808

After the death of his father in 1883, Paul inherited a considerable fortune, which allowed him to resign from his post as the Prefecture Councilor of Evreux. He abandoned his job with pleasure, stating that he "felt much more drawn to the refined tastes of an artist, a collector, a man of letters, than to the troubled world of politics or the narrow world of public service." At twenty-seven years old, he was able to devote his time exclusively to his passion: the history of the Consulate and the Empire, especially Tuscany under Napoleonic rule. Tireless traveler, he visited Holland, Poland, Egypt, Russia, and Spain on many occasions, but Paul remained partial to Italy. Throughout his travels, he amassed considerable documentation that he kept at his home in Boulogne, which is today the Library Marmottan. Information in these archives supported many of his publications, including *Le Royaume d'Etrurie (1801-1807)*, *Bonaparte et la République de Lucques (1801-1805)*, *Les troupes de Joseph Napoléon en Espagne*, and *Elisa Bonaparte*.

Louis Gauffier
Portrait of an Officer from the Cisalpine Republic
1801, oil on canvas

François-Xavier Fabre, *Portrait of the Duchesse de Feltre*, 1810, oil on canvas

Louis Gauffier, *The Salucci Family*, 1800, oil on canvas

Louis Gauffier, *The Arno Valley Seen from the Paradisino of Vallombrosa*, 1799, oil on canvas

Johann Henrich Schmidt, *Murat Giving the Order to Take Capri*, 1808, oil on canvas

Paris

Etienne Bouhot
The Courtyard of the Institut de France
oil on canvas

While researching the history of these kingdoms, principalities, and dukedoms, which were often governed by members of Napoleon's family, Paul Marmottan also collected numerous works about Paris and its surroundings under the Empire and the Consulate. He wrote many articles on the chateaux of Neuilly, Passy, Villiers, and Bagetelle, a First Empire hunting lodge. Part of his collection of paintings, engravings, and drawings relates

Jacques Swebach
Equipage in the Courtyard of Neuilly Chateau
1810, oil on canvas

Joseph Eusèbe Prévot
View of Pont Neuf
ca. 1846, oil on canvas

to his research. The titles of several artworks confirm the close relationship between his writings and his collection: *Equipage in the Courtyard of Neuilly Chateau, The Gallery of Wood at the Palais Royal, View of the Gates at the Faubourg Saint-Martin, View of Pont Neuf, Chateau de la Chaussée at Bougival* as well as other landscapes of Paris and its environs executed by Bouhot, Swebach, Bertin and Demarne.

Studios

These two studio scenes illustrate artistic life during the Second Restoration.

Adrienne Grandpierre-Deverzy painted the studio of her husband, Abel de Pujol, three times. Pujol was a pupil of David and the recipient of the 1811 Prix de Rome. He had a very successful career decorating churches and public monuments. He was also a professor, and gave lessons to young noblewomen.

The second studio is that of Baron Gros, Auguste Masse's teacher. The studio is located in the French Institute, whose copula is visible. After David's exile in 1815, Gros continued to work in his style. He is seen here surrounded by his students. Gros placed a model of a medallion of David on the left wall to pay homage to his master.

Adrienne Marie Louise Grandpierre-Deverzy
The Studio of Abel de Pujol
1822, oil on canvas

Auguste Antoine Masse
Inside the Studio of Gros
1824, oil on canvas

Portraits

Paul Marmottan also conducted several studies of French painters who were active in the period between the Treaty of Versailles and the July Revolution, especially Louis and François Watteau and Louis Boilly—whose work he acquired twenty-six oil paintings and six drawings. In the introduction of his publication *L'Ecole française de peinture (1780-1830)*, he noted *"above all, we dedicated ourselves to present a sincere judgment, proud of our independence, relying on a long and conscientious study*

Joseph Franque
Portrait Bonaparte, First Consul
ca. 1799, oil on canvas

original artworks." He collected many portraits of Napoleon, members of his family, and high dignitaries of the regime, such as *Portrait of Bonaparte, First Consul* by Franque, *Jérôme Bonaparte* by Kinson, *Portrait of Désirée Clary*, the future Queen of Sweden, by the Baron Gérard and *Joachim Murat Giving the Order to Take Capri in 1808* by Schmidt.

Baron François Gérard
Portrait of Désirée Clary
1810, oil on canvas

Henri François Riesener
Portrait of François-Joseph Talma
1824, oil on canvas

Robert Lefévre
Portrait of Jean-Victor Bertin
1805, oil on canvas

François Joseph Kinson
Catherine of Wurtenberg, Queen of Westphalia
1810, oil on canvas

Decorative Arts

Marmottan collected furniture and bronze statues, including some of the highest quality models, at a time when a taste for the Middle Ages, the Renaissance, and the eighteenth century still dominated. Often executed for Napoleon or the imperial family, these objects once adorned the palaces at the Tuileries, Fontainebleau, Malmaison, Versailles, and Compiègne. This exceptional collection includes a large *surtout de table* in gilt bronze signed by Pierre Philippe Thomire, the Prince of Tallyrand's *Chandelier with Musicians*, girandoles by Rabiat, candelabras by Feuchère, the Duchess of Berry's *Geographic Clock* from the factory of Sèvres, imitation porphyry vases in porcelain from the Sarreguemines workshops, mahogany seats signed by the Jacob Brothers, Jacob Desmalter, Bernard Molitor, neo-Egyptian consoles, a desk by Pierre-Antoine Bellangé, as well as marble busts of the imperial family signed by Bosio, Laurent Bartolini and Delaistre.

François-Honoré Georges Jacob-Desmalter
Writing Desk with Cupboard
1805, mahogany
Bronze panels depicting Venus anadyomene and Flora.

Anonymous
Clock, Eagle Vase
ca. 1800, gilt bronze

Anonymous
Fear of the Dog
ca. 1810, gilt bronze

Italian Pedestal Table
ca. 1800, bronze and painted stucco
In the center is Bacchus as a child on his chariot carrying
two small satyrs.

◁

Factory of Sevres
Geographic Clock
1813-1821
This clock was designed in 1813 to honor Napoleon's glories.
It was altered after the fall of the Empire. The twelve historical
scenes on the shield-shaped dial were replaced with scenes
evocative of different time zones. The bust of Napoleon was
replaced by Diane and Apollo. The top of the clock turns,
showing the face of Apollo during the day and that of Diane
during the night. In 1822, the clock was acquired by Louis
XVIII and offered to the Duchess of Berry for her chateau at
Rosny.

The Circle of Claude Monet
The Impressionists

The history of the most celebrated artistic movement of all times began in the mid-nineteenth century. But the group was not named the Impressionists until 1874, when Monet showed his painting of Le Havre harbor at the famous exhibition in the studio of the photographer Nadar.

Many artists participated in the exhibition with Monet: Berthe Morisot, Degas, Cézanne, Guillaumin, Pissarro, Renoir, Sisley. Rebelling against the official Salon system, these artists fought for new pictorial freedom. Impressionism was born. Thanks to several generous donations from Victorine de Monchy, the daughter of Dr. de Bellio; Michel Monet, the son of the painter; and the artist Henri Duhem, the museum proudly presents exceptional artworks by the artistic elite from this period. The Musée Marmottan Monet owns the world's largest collection of artworks by Claude Monet: from the sketches of his youth to the water lilies of Giverny. It is an exceptional collection that attests to his mesmerizing life.

Claude Monet
Impression, Sunrise
1873, oil on canvas

First Encounters Beside Water

Monet grew up in the mid-nineteenth century in Le Havre, one of France's largest commercial harbors. Oscar, as he was called then, was not really interested in school. During the long hours of class, he sketched portraits. These drawings were exhibited in the window of an art supply store when a

Johann Jongkind, *Port Vendre*, 1880, watercolor

Claude Monet, *Dandy with a Cigar*, 1857, heightened drawing

painter noticed them. Shortly thereafter, he invited Monet to come with him and experience the pleasures of painting in the open air.

Thus, thanks to Eugène Boudin, Monet discovered his first *seaside panoramas*. As an adult, these scenes became an *obsession*, and he would continually

attempt to capture their beauty. Monet never forgot these long walks and the *revelation, the light had just burst forth*. [Marc Elder: *At Claude Monet's Home in Giverny*, Paris, 1924]

In Normandy, he also met the Dutch painter Johann Jongkind, who helped him to complete his training. Quickly, the three became an inseparable trio—a friendship that Monet would always remember. At Honfleur, Trouville, and Etretat, Monet tried his hand at landscapes, painted a few seaside panoramas, and sketched young women wearing hoopskirts and walking along the beach. Although he soon left Le Havre, Monet often returned there *to reimmerse himself in the sea air*. [Letter from Monet to Mr. Joyant, Giverny, February 8, 1896]

Eugène Boudin, *On the Beach*. 1863, watercolor and pastel

Paris and Its Surroundings

Paris attracted prominent artists of the time; furthermore, it was the place to take the classes that artists gave in their studios. In Paris in 1859, Monet met Pissarro, then Renoir, Bazille, and Sisley. Abandoned by the conservative establishment, they shared for a few years the torments of isolation and, for some, destitution. Despite their common attraction to nature, the capital offered these young painters numerous motifs. Worm's-eye views,

Claude Monet
The Tuileries Gardens
1876, oil on canvas

bird's-eye studies, like in this scene of *The Tuileries Gardens* bathed in sunlight.

Through *his train stations*, Monet depicted modern times, the wonders of progress, and the machines that allowed some to access the city with its business and spectacles, and enabled others to relax for a few hours on Sunday in the country. Concealing the harshness of the laborers' work and the unavoidable nuisances, he transformed the machines' repugnant fumes into floating scrolls of smoke that sputtered under the imposing metal framework of the Pont de l'Europe.

But the new Paris—with its buildings, gardens, and vibrant architecture under various light effects, did not fully satisfy Monet. The refusal of his works by the Salon confirmed his opinion, *...don't you believe that, in front of only nature, we would do better*, he wrote to Bazille. He preferred the verdant banks of the Seine outside of the city to the quays of Paris. When he lived in Argenteuil, his friends visited him often, and together, they painted days in the country. We can imagine Jean, Monet's eldest son, and his mother Camille walking in the fields while the artist was at his easel.

Claude Monet
The Pont de l'Europe, Gare Saint-Lazare
1877, oil on canvas

Monet With His Family

The young and graceful Camille Donicieux was Monet's first model. She posed for *The Woman in the Green Dress*, which was accepted by the Salon of 1866. The next year, she gave birth to Jean; eleven years later, she had Michel. With Monet, she

Claude Monet, *Jean*, 1880 and *Michel,* 1883

Auguste Renoir, *Madame Claude Monet*
1872, oil on canvas

shared years of poverty, and consented to the long periods of solitude that the life of the young artist imposed upon them. During the summer of 1878, in order to spend as little money as possible, the Monets shared a house with the Hoschedés. The families met when Ernest Hoschedé, a successful merchant and important collector, commissioned the artist for his Chateau of Montgeron. Financial woes triggered the liquidation of Hoshedé's

property, and motivated the two families to live together. Horschedé's wife, Alice, took care of everyone, especially Camille who was in poor health. After a long illness, Camille passed away in 1879 in the house at Vétheuil. Frequently left alone by her husband, Alice decided to stay with Monet and to take care of the children. Together, they looked for a new home.

Claude Monet
Walk Near Argenteuil
1873, oil on canvas

Claude Monet
Water Lilies
1916-1919, oil on canvas (Detail)

The Enchantment of Giverny

After a short stay in Poissy, they finally discovered Giverny.

From his youth in Le Havre until his move to Giverny, Monet changed his address several times, but he never really left the Seine with all of its twists and turns. In 1883, wanting to *get away from this horrible, ill-fated Poissy*, he and Alice explored the region of Vernon. Along a tributary of the Seine, Monet discovered a small village with three hundred inhabitants. With its hilly backdrop, green prairies, surrounding marshes, and flower orchards, the location seduced Monet. The next month, Monet and Alice rented a house there. Monet lived there for forty-three years, which were full of joy and tragedy. He arranged his new home and settled in with his large family as best as he could. In addition to Jean and Michel, he was taking care of Alice's six children. This period was still difficult, but promising. Immediately, Monet began gardening. Over the course of the alterations, plantings, and seasons, the garden became a work of art by Master of Giverny, his most beautiful source of inspiration, and the very essence of his paintings.

Claude Monet
Water Lilies. Evening Effect.
1897-1898, oil on canvas (Detail)

Travelling

Quickly, life was organized. Alice managed the household; the two youngest children went to the village school, the eldest studied at boarding school, while Monet fully indulged in his passions for horticulture and painting. He shaped his garden, playing with the colors of the flowers, the sizes of the trees, and the weather's frosts. But, his thirst for discovery was never satisfied. Monet artist started several paintings, always representing the same subject differently. Then, the next day, he chose the painting that best corresponded to that very instant to continue his work and depict what he was seeing as accurately as possible.

While the new iron and glass materials once thrilled Claude Monet, during this time he loved to observe light reflecting on stone. For two years

Claude Monet
Tulip Field in Holland
1886, oil on canvas

needed to find new lights and other impressions. Unknown horizons attracted him; trips were necessary. The first was to Italy, along the French border, to a small village that Monet originally discovered with Renoir where he returned alone to work. The lush vegetation and *the enchanted country* inspired several paintings. Then he visited Holland and spent some time in Antibes, Juan-les-Pins, and the French region of la Creuse with its *terrible wilderness*. This was the beginning of his series: haystacks, poplars, and the cathedral. On the same day, the

he *dug* to reproduce the majestic façade of Rouen Cathedral. It was such a difficult task that sometimes he found himself on the brink of ruin. He wrote to his companion, *…I am shattered…, I've had a night full of nightmares: the cathedral was falling on top of me, it seemed either blue or pink or yellow…* A harmony of white, brown, and blue—a series of 30 versions were executed, 20 of which would be exhibited in 1895 at the gallery of the important dealer, Paul Durand-Ruel. They received glowing reviews.

Sunlight Effects. End of Day 1892

How can the artist, only a few centimeters away from his canvas, understand an effect that is both subtle and precise, which can only be appreciated from a distance? This is the disconcerting mystery of his eye. The eye of Monet, precursor, precedes us and guides us through a visual evolution…

[Georges Clemenceau, *La Justice*, May 20, 1895]

Claude Monet
Rouen Cathedral. Sunlight Effects. End of Day
1892, oil on canvas

Before the exhibition, Monet left his loved ones to go on an extended journey to meet his stepson in Norway. It was the height of winter. In the

Claude Monet, *Mount Kolsaas in Norway*
1895, oil on canvas

beginning, Monet was dazzled by the *enormous frozen waterfalls*, sizeable lakes consumed by ice, and gigantic pine forests where *large bears* lived. But then

came moments of doubt. It was too difficult to settle in and paint in such a cold region, he hesitated to return home. However, *this white immensity*, which he discovered in Sandviken, near Oslo, inspired another, much different series: The Mount Kolsaas.

Four years later, Monet went to England. He was familiar with the country. In 1871 he went to the English coast to avoid enlistment. Monet brought back with him some landscapes, and especially the desire to return there to paint the *fog effects on the Thames*.

In 1899, he embarked upon three consecutive trips to London. Almost one hundred works by Monet are devoted to it. Parliament, Charing Cross Bridge and Waterloo Bridge—three pictures for a single purpose: to paint the transparency and the lightness of the fog pierced by the sun's rays as it enveloped the monuments, dissolving their outlines.

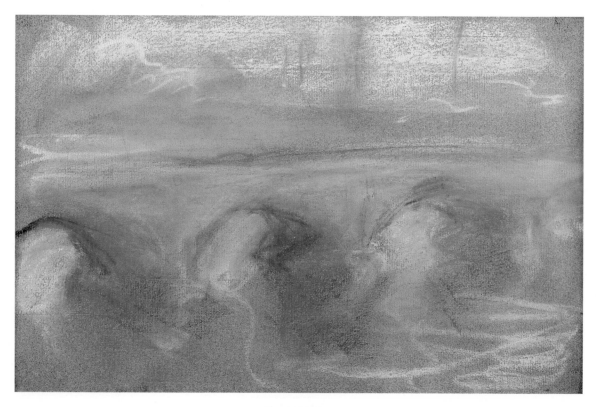

Claude Monet
Waterloo Bridge
1900, pastel

The Thames was golden, god it was beautiful, so I started
to work furiously, following the sun and its reflections
on the water...

[Claude Monet to Alice, London, Sunday, February 3, 1901]

Claude Monet
London, Houses of Parliament
1900-1901, oil on canvas

The Flowers of Giverny

The time for travel passed. The artist got older and solitude did not suit Alice. His time away had to be brief and was not really profitable. Despite the delight that he felt after a day in front of the beauty of nature, with the sun's brilliance, the magnificent scenes and the harmonious places, Monet was exasperated that he could not be close to those he loved. In addition, he did not have the atmosphere, or the necessary light to create enough paintings to eliminate his financial problems. In 1890, with the help of his dealer, Paul Durand-Ruel, he was able to buy Giverny. He was completely happy there, and little by little, his garden became the source for all of his artwork. In 1893, he acquired a plot of land next to his property, on the other side of the railroad tracks. Village officials accepted Monet's request to use water from the Epte River to create a pond for *the pleasure for the eyes* and *new pictures to be painted*. It was simple yet magnificent at the same time. Surrounded by irises, weeping willows, ash trees, and with large floating lily pads, the pond provided the Master with many impressions from which to work.

Gardens on land, gardens in the water, Monet did

Claude Monet
Yellow and Purple Irises
1924-1925, oil on canvas

not rest until he perfected them. He constantly ordered flowers and small trees from the biggest nurseries. During his travels, he always tried to discover new species and have them delivered. In his absence, Alice had to follow instructions; above all she had to take *good care of his dear flowers*. Every spring it was dazzling with the blooming of the trees and bunches of flowers that were overflowing with colors.

It is a realm colored and perfumed by flowers. Every month, new flowers decorate, from the lilacs and irises to the chrysanthemums and nasturtiums. Roses of Sharon, forget-me-nots, violets—spectacular and simple flowers mingled, and followed one another on this always thriving land… under the infallible eye of the master.
[Gustave Geffroy, *Monet, sa vie, son œuvre*, Macula editions, 1980]

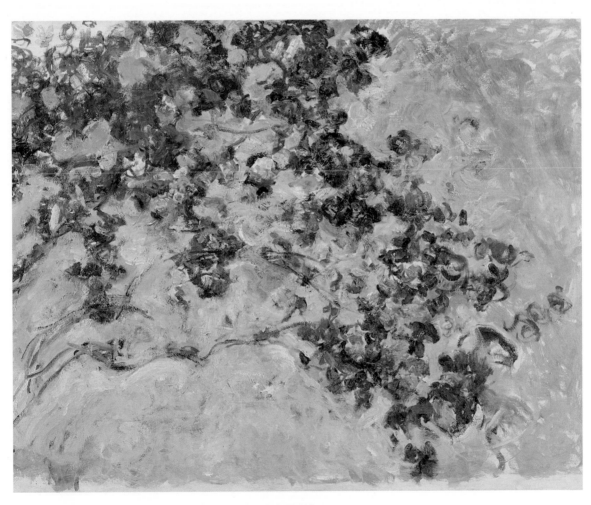

Claude Monet
Roses
1925-1926, oil on canvas (Detail)

The Dazzling Conquest of Light

On the water's surface, water lilies carried by their powerful foliage, motionlessly await the fulfillment of destinies. A dignified subject for meditation. Since there is neither frame, nor beginning, nor end, we can only catch the sight at the moment when it happens to find its development from painting to painting.

[Georges Clemenceau, *Claude Monet*, Perrin editions, 2000]

Claude Monet
The Water Lily Pond
1917-1919, oil on canvas

From One Bank to Another

A small wooden bridge was built, which reminds us of Monet's interest in Japanese prints. In 1899, he still painted a very realistic series of it. After 1918, the lines of the Japanese bridge, like those of the overhanging arch, disintegrate into a profusion of vibrant brushstrokes that fill the canvas, to better reproduce the abundant vegetation.

Claude Monet
The Japanese Bridge
1918, oil on canvas

Claude Monet
The Japanese Bridge
1918-1924, oil on canvas

[…] A curving bridge, in the shape of those found in Hiroshige's landscapes, gives access to this place of illusions…On the rails of this bridge, wisteria plants climb and they hang down in bunches, in multicolored stalactites, the tips coming to meet their mirror images in the Epte […].

[Arsène Alexandre, *Claude Monet*, 1921]

Going Towards the House

The path that leads to the house was bordered by spruce and cypress trees. Monet did not like the shadow they created. Despite Alice's enthusiasm to save them, they were cut down and the path was

richness of the colors equals the density of the vegetation. The result is enduring and almost violent, similar to life.

Dramatic events upset Monet during his time at

Claude Monet
The House Viewed from the Rose Garden
1922-1924, oil on canvas

recovered by arches that were soon adorned with flowers. In 1922, Monet painted this site in the same fiery tones with the *House Viewed from the Rose Garden*. While the *green and floral vault* was dark, *the sun's blazes* set the sky and the leaves aglow with red tones that filled the house. The thickness of the paint, the abundance of the brushstrokes, and the

Giverny. He was deeply affected by the death of his beloved Alice, as well as the loss of his eldest son in 1914. He spent the war alone at Giverny. The threat of blindness haunted him and, in 1923, it forced him to undergo an operation which he kept delaying. He was not satisfied with the outcome until July 1925.

[…]My vision is completely improved… he wrote in
July 1925 to A. Barbier. Then in October, he con-
fided in G. Berheim-Jeune, *[…]I am pleased to have
finally recovered the sight of colors. It is a real revival.*

Claude Monet
The Path Under the Rose Arches
1920-1922, oil on canvas (Detail)

In the *Pink Mortared Roughcast* House *at the End of the Garden*

The House at Giverny

Eugène Delacroix
*Tiger Frightened
by a Snake*
1858, pen and
Indian ink

Like the pink facade, chosen by the former owner who was homesick for Guadeloupe, the colors of the rooms of the house were as bright as Monet's palette. Sky-blue for the kitchen and the small sitting room, very bright yellow for the dining room where the large family and a few of the privileged guests ate around the big table. Some of the most beautiful Japanese prints, which Monet collected since 1871, hung on the walls. The artist worked in the sitting room/studio where he also liked to read

with Alice. His works filled the walls. There was not enough space, so a second studio was quickly built in 1899 in the outbuildings. Sixteen years later, in 1915, a third studio was built for Monet's work on the *Giant Decorations*, a collection of paintings he wished to offer to the State. The roof was made of steel and glass to give the painter the full daylight. The furnishings were sparse; the entire space was devoted to his work on the immense canvases that Clemenceau would soon call marvels.

The second floor of the house was reserved for bedrooms, whose decoration was only seen by close friends. Here Monet displayed his collection of artworks. Sometimes he bought or exchanged works, but frequently they were given to him. Everything was shown. Watercolors by Delacroix, drawings by Constantin Guys as well as oils by Cézanne, Corot, Boudin, Renoir, Morisot, and two bronze sculptures by Rodin.

Gustave Caillebotte
Paris Street in the Rain
1877, oil on canvas
This work was given by Caillebotte to Claude Monet, who hung it above his bed. Both shared a love of flowers and gardening. They exchanged cuttings and opinions.

Around Monet

Few friendships compare to the one Monet had with Renoir during their youth. It was *a part of my life*, filled with the first studios where they had to submit to the master's dogma, then getaways in the Fontainebleau forest, and later, days of painting at his house in Argenteuil. Several works from this period remain, such as the wonderful pendant for the portrait of Camille, *Monet Reading*, where he is smoking his pipe.

Auguste Renoir
Monet Reading
1872, oil on canvas

In addition to the large collection left to the museum by the son of the Master of Giverny, other dazzling artworks by Monet and his friends, as well as works by artists from the periods before and after Impressionism, enrich the museum's prominent collection, and contribute to its fame.

A canvas by Camille Corot, given to the museum by Nelly Sergeant-Duhem, reminds us that already, the ephemeral daylight interested this painter who worked in the open air. The colors used in this scene *through the leaves* are as delicate as the careful execution.

This extraordinary exotic still-life with brilliant colors was painted by Paul Gauguin in 1897 during his second stay in Tahiti.

Camille Corot
The Pont of Ville d'Avray
1871, oil on canvas

Paul Gauguin
Bouquet of Flowers
1897, oil on canvas

Sisley, Pissarro, Guillaumin and Many Others...

[...]hounded, shunned, banned by official art, these three artists with Monet, Renoir, Degas and Berthe Morisot, were the directors of a new school... a few young men and one young woman who have caused the jury to tremble for the past five to six years [...] wrote the art critic Castagnary about the 1874 exhibition at Nadar's studio.

Alfred Sisley
Spring in the Environs of Paris. Apple Trees in Bloom
1897, oil on canvas

It was not until the early twentieth century that Monet's talent was recognized, soon after, his genius was acknowledged. Alfred Sisley was not as fortunate. His fame was achieved posthumously. After his death, Monet contributed to the purchase of a few of his studio works to help support Sisley's destitute children.

Camille Pissarro achieved some success, but never enough to take advantage of his fame. He alternated several styles to suit the subject as well as his appetite for discovery. This scene of a Parisian boulevard under the snow is painted almost at the same point of view as the figures. Delicately executed, the painting is bathed in a gray tone covered with bits of white, which are almost transparent and as light as snowflakes. The cold seems biting, looking at the small figures that clearly stand out from the scene.

Armand Guillaumin was a faithful participant in the Impressionist exhibitions. Early on in his career, he painted numerous scenes of the suburbs where he inserted sad social realities. Gradually, other French landscapes inspired his lively and colorful canvases. He brought back from the French region of la Creuse a powerful series that prefigured the brilliant light of Fauvism. In 1894, Geoffroy called the series *fireworks that burst from his palette*.

Camille Pissarro, *The Outer Boulevards. Snow Effects*. 1879, oil on canvas

Armand Guillaumin
The Creuse at Genetin
ca. 1900, oil on canvas

Albert Lebourg
Place de la Concorde
Oil on canvas

The fame of some painters should not obscure the
talent of other artists who also deserve recognition,
such as Albert Lebourg, and from the next genera-
tion, Paul Signac, Henri Lebasque and Henri Le
Sidaner. Some of them knew the *Intransigents* of
painting, and even participated in Impressionist
exhibitions. At the fringes of Impressionism, each
tried different pictorial approaches and flirted
with different techniques. One moved towards
Symbolism, while others towards Fauvism and
even Pointillism. But they all had something in
common: a love of nature and light.

Landscape painter, Albert Lebourg often painted
the countryside, which he adored, like the banks
of the Seine and Vernon in winter. He also
painted ravishing scenes of Paris.

*One penetrates into a world of infinite softness, of a
delightful brightness, of a harmony where energies
evaporate into a silvery atmosphere...* wrote Gustave
Geoffroy about the painter's large retrospective
in 1918.

Paul Signac, twenty years his junior, had great
esteem for Claude Monet:

Henri Lebasque
Young Girl Reading
Oil on canvas

[…] I've been painting for two years and my only models have been your works; I followed the wonderful path that you opened for us […] Signac wrote in the 1880s.

[J. Rewald, *Histoire de l'impressionnisme*, Albin Michel editions, 1955]

Paul Signac, *Departure of the Terre-Neuviers.* 1928, watercolor

As for Le Sidaner, after a Symbolist period where dreams and the imagination brought him to nostalgic environments, he began to paint in his garden like the Master of Giverny. In Gerberoy, a small village in Oise, Le Sidaner abandoned figure painting. For almost forty years, he represented only his flowers, his house, and the charming scenes from life that unfolded there, an enchanting world.

Henri Le Sidaner
River Bordered by Trees
1923, oil on canvas

Berthe Morisot
Denis and Annie Rouart Foundation

[…]never has a soul or spirit shown the depth of its reverie and the strength of its spiritual willpower with more intensity than this lively and delicate artist devoted to conquering the complexity of reality and the poetry of truth.

GUSTAVE GEFFROY

Berthe Morisot
On the Lakeside
1883, oil on canvas

Denis Rouart, the grandson of Berthe Morisot, was married to Anne-Marie Conan, who donated over seventy artworks by Morisot as well as paintings by Edgar Degas, Edouard Manet, Claude Monet, Auguste Renoir, and Henri Rouart, among others, to the Musée Marmottan Monet. Curator of the Musée de Nancy, Denis Rouart, honored the memory of Morisot, like his mother Julie Manet. With his wife, he helped to organize exhibitions of Morisot's work and wrote numerous publications about her art.

From a very early age, Berthe Morisot devoted herself to painting.

Advised by the best professors, like Camille Corot, who introduced her to the joy of painting in the open air, Berthe courageously followed her dreams, at a time when the world of art was still very much a masculine domain.

She had numerous friends with whom she corresponded frequently: Puvis de Chavannes, Monet, Renoir, Degas, and Mallarmé.

Most of her close friends were members of the Impressionists, a movement that was baptized in 1874 at the *First Impressionist Exhibition*, in which Morisot participated.

She married Eugène Manet, brother of the famous painter, and gave birth to their daughter, Julie, who became her favorite model.

Throughout her short life, during periods of serenity and doubt, Berthe Morisot knew how to combine her painting with her life as a woman.

Berthe Morisot
Eugène Manet on the Isle of Wight
1875, oil on canvas

Berthe Morisot by Edouard Manet

Berthe Morisot copied paintings by the Old Masters at the Louvre. It was there, in 1867, that Fantin-Latour introduced her to the already famous painter, Edouard Manet, whose talent and temperament she admired. As early as 1868, Manet asked her to pose for him. He painted her ten times, showing Morisot's remarkable beauty, and each portrait allows us to discover another facet of her personality, which combines delicacy and violence, melancholy and ardor. Manet never painted Berthe Morisot with a paintbrush in her hand, although a few years later, he offered her an encouraging present as a token of his esteem for her work: an easel.

They had a close friendship, and while Berthe Morisot was not Manet's student, she was certainly influenced by *this bit of new technique, this new way of painting*, and his genius.

After Manet's death, Berthe Morisot actively participated in the retrospective exhibition that preceded the sale of his artworks. The exhibition was organized, in accordance with the terms of the painter's will, by Theodore Duret, a writer and critic who was Manet's friend.

Edouard Manet
Portrait of Berthe Morisot Reclining
1873, oil on canvas

The Year 1874

This was a decisive time in the artist's life. Extremely saddened by the death of her father, Morisot took refuge in her work. In the spring, she made the important decision to abandon the official Salon to join a group of independent artists that had just been created. Morisot accepted Degas's invitation to hang her paintings in Nadar's large studio, thus participating in the First Impressionist Exhibition.

On December 22, 1874, Berthe married Eugène Manet at the church of Passy. In 1878, the couple had a daughter, Julie.

Male figures are rare in Morisot's artwork. Nevertheless, she occasionally represented her husband in the company of their daughter as in the painting, Eugène Manet and his Daughter in the Garden at Bougival.

At every age, Julie was her favorite model, drawn so often in her sketchbooks, inside on a sofa, or perched on a ladder picking cherries.

Berthe Morisot
Eugène Manet and His Daughter in the Garden at Bougival
1881, oil on canvas

Berthe Morisot
The Cherry Tree
1891, oil on canvas

Depicting Travel

Berthe Morisot
Nice Harbor
1882, oil on paper backed with canvas

Berthe Morisot loved traveling.

She and her husband often got away from Paris to discover new landscapes and start new paintings. The intense light, vast panoramas, exotic vegetation, hot and colorful atmosphere drew the artist to Nice, especially the old part of the town. She visited there several times.

She brought back many works from Nice. Several seascapes, like *Nice Harbor* from 1882, were executed in a very assertive manner, with almost fierce brushstrokes. *Nice Harbor* is a novel composition where the subject is placed in the top portion of the canvas.

No matter what the subject or medium, everything was a pretext to explore the effects of light and emotion. With pastels and especially watercolors, Berthe Morisot captured numerous ephemeral moments playing with brightness, colors, and, as always, with the effects of transparency and lightness.

Art historian Claude Roger-Marx wrote, *Nowhere does Berthe Morisot appear more personal, more exquisite, and never, in fact, will there ever be… so close a correlation between the quality of the expeditious, instantaneous process, and the very nature of the artist, all in the first stoke.*

Berthe Morisot
White Boat in Nice Harbor
1881, watercolor

Auguste Renoir

Berthe Morisot
Children at the Basin
1886, oil on canvas

The friendship between Berthe Morisot and Auguste Renoir began in their youth. As a member of the Impressionists, he defended the movement and was a loyal companion. Renoir often attended the delightful Thursday dinners organized by Berthe Morisot where painters, poets, and musicians, among others, gathered. Morisot admired Renoir's painting. Deeply moved while visiting his studio in 1886, she wrote in her notebook *overall, he is an artist of natural elegance, a refined person, a great draughtsman, as well as a colorist of the most exquisite sensations…*

At the request of the Manets, Renoir painted his first portrait of Julie at age of 8, in their living room with a cat on her knees. A few years later, when Julie was mourning the death of her father, he depicted the young girl wearing a black velvet dress.

Auguste Renoir
Portrait of Julie Manet
1898, oil on canvas

Comrade in Arms

Present at every Impressionist Exhibition (except the year her daughter was born), Morisot was considered by her peers as a *comrade in arms* and essential to the movement. Everyone appreciated her charms and admired her talent.

On March 2, 1895, at only 53 years old, Berthe Morisot passed away.

In early 1896, to pay her the tribute her life and work, the *Intransigeants* organized the most comprehensive exhibition of her art at Durand-Ruel's gallery. Stéphane Mallarmé wrote the preface to the catalogue; Degas, Monet, and Renoir hung the artwork.

The exhibition was a success and the reviews were glowing. Thadée Natanson, journalist for the *Revue Blanche* wrote:

As much as one has ever tried to define the appearance of an artwork or one of its qualities in words, this time, one loses any desire to do so. Here, one has to refrain from

Berthe Morisot
The Castle Mount
1888, watercolor

entrusting to them the task of evoking anything of the charm and the enchantment of this or even anything that could claim to do so. Their bouquets would here be discolored and faded.

Berthe Morisot
Young Girl Leaning on her Elbows
1887, red chalk

Berthe Morisot
Girl in a Blue Jersey
1886, pastel on canvas

Acknowledgments

Mr. Arnaud d'HAUTERIVES,
Permanent Secretary of the Académie des Beaux-Arts

Mr. Jean-Marie GRANIER,
Member of the French Academy, Director of the Paul Marmottan Foundation and Musée Marmottan Monet

Mrs. Nadège MONNÉGER and Mr. François DESFACHELLE for their collaboration